Edu-babble

The Glamorous World of the New York City Public School System

Gwendolyn Green

authorHOUSE®

AuthorHouse™
1663 Liberty Drive, Suite 200
Bloomington, IN 47403
www.authorhouse.com
Phone: 1-800-839-8640

First published by AuthorHouse 4/16/2009

ISBN: 978-1-4343-6062-5 (sc)

Library of Congress Control Number: 2009901620

Printed in the United States of America
Bloomington, Indiana

This book is printed on acid-free paper.

To my friend Chris

This Manual to Success Is What Key be to Lock

I think the worst thing about a book is redundancy. Many of my friends told me to "flesh" this book out. But then, it would not be what I imagine my dear friend and former coworker Chris should have read before he walked into our school...and quickly out again. Lasting 4 months at the school, he was the third of ten newbie's to quit that year. Being a newbie is tough. A guide to the sometimes bizzaro world of New York City public schools is what he needed. I'm not going to say, "Don't get me wrong, I love my job." No, I enjoy helping children and I do to an amazing degree. We share with them what we know but the most enjoyable part is discovering the world together. You cannot imagine how gratifying it is to help a child accomplish something they never thought they could do. Nevertheless, being an employee of bureaucracy-ridden New York City is what puts the weight on your shoulders.

I could have become a politician, a doctor, a lawyer, a social worker, or work for the Red Cross. I thought long and hard about how those jobs are repairing the damage done. I wanted to get to the skin before it was cut with disenfranchisement. Maybe I could make the skin tougher. I could help by preventing. To get to the root of the problem I would have to start when the people were young.

Yes, this is all non-fiction so put down that Teaching Fellows application and read on. I'm positive that you will wonder why the lid hasn't been blown off this yet… it's gone beyond the realm of tragedy and into comedy. Sure, our chancellor has a chauffeur and our students get to eat a slice of Ellio's pizza and drink a pint of grade D milk for the one meal they are guaranteed that day… but he needs it. He has important business to attend to. How can he overhaul our way of teaching every two years without being driven up Park Avenue and home to either of his $2 million apartments both at luxury building 565 Park Avenue in Manhattan?

The demands put on the teachers by the government are difficult. It is felt nation wide but the New York City system is unique in that our officials try very hard to fix things. Every year there is a new focus of study. Every two years, a whole new system of teaching. Every three years, a whole new distribution of leadership. If you're not "with it" then you're more confused than Borat. "Whats up Vanilla face?" This is the problem with new teachers. Whether you just framed that B.A. in education, got assigned by TFA, or getting back in the game after cranking out a couple of kids… "the times, they are a- changin'."

"Ms. Green, I will arrange our post-observation as soon as I finish your rubric. Can you remind me which graphic organizer you distributed to the higher-level students? I was busy documenting how many charts of progress you have hanging in your classroom. Oh, hold on, there is an announcement. *May I have your attention please? Attention workers, the new lesson plan format will be in your mailboxes today to implement the Johnny Johnson's Journey to Jubilation program criteria. Your students will be tested on the national standards of ELA and Math. Now, I know some of your seventh graders are reading on a third grade level but that shouldn't hinder their learning. Some guidelines that are mandatory to follow include differentiating, modeling, and snitching."*

These terms, this way of talking, is what we like to refer to as "Edu-babble." Orwell liked to call it doublespeak. Edu-babble is just that, with some hip catchphrases attached. And by hip I mean impractical.

Three Matters of Concern

* = Amendment or addition to the rule

1. Building Strong Personal Relationships with Colleagues is Key

- it will give you backup when you need it and it will assist you with the challenging task of being a newbie

- everything falls into place after you have accomplished this

How to Do It:

1. Never talk to, about, and around anyone about the topics of school unless you are positive of the other person's feelings on the matter:

❖   My classmate from college turned colleague... was exposed as the principal's nephew. I spent 6 months of slaughtering the rationality of the admin and providing lesson plans to this under qualified peer until I sniffed the stench of gossip. Next thing I know, the spy is spotted. An unnerving stare will cut a conversation short in the staff lounge. A quick eye glance produces a sly alarm to the other. An awkwardness (of approximately 3 seconds which will feel like an eternity) will occur until a savior changes the subject away from the sensitive topic.

2. Don't get angry at anyone who is just doing their job

❖   I've heard administrators publicly tell staff that at least one category must be checked off in the unsuitable column on the evaluation. First, the admin can present a black and white copy of the flaw they are assisting you with. Second, the admin can maximize or minimize that flaw depending on their agenda.

> * if they do in fact have a personal vendetta
> against you, then use your hate to drive
> your motivation to get shit done

3. Don't become associated with the first people who want to be your friend. Why do they want your friendship? Maybe they don't have any friends of their own...and you can bank on there being a very good reason for that.

❖   On the Friday before the school year begins, the teachers are given their definite program for the year. Then, a dignified rush to horde all the furniture and text books you can get. Simply calling a teacher desk yours is not enough. Taping your name to it in front of witnesses is a better idea. Oh, and acquire as many filing cabinets otherwise your crap will be on display or worse...you will have to use your teacher's choice money on

4. Always use your manners and be polite. Introduce yourself and always be the one to ask how someone's day is going.

❖   Mr. Gomez doesn't do a damn thing in social studies except worksheets and movies due to the distant days of teaching in the honeymoon phase, when he was able to wrestle the bureaucracy. I think at his retirement party there couldn't be a roast because he is so beloved. I wish I could ask him the ingredients to the spell he casts. Of course, that would break Rule # 1.

5. make mental notes of dirt on everyone in the building, especially your administrators, so they seem less intimidating:

❖   This old biddy told me one day how she had "relations" with a snooty higher- up, from then on the pedestal was lowered…smooth sailing

    * earn a reputation as keeping your mouth shut

6. hang out with anyone over 50 because they are the ones retiring in a couple of years and don't care who they rat on

❖   In one year, I learned the whole history of my school (1975- present) by chatting with the old biddies

7. be friendly in the off hours with the people who offer life saving solutions for those occasional but detrimental problems

❖   i.e. Grace the attendance/coverage lady and Betty the paycheck/retirement fund/ health insurance lady

8. if someone goes out of their way to track you down during their busy day then make their issue a top priority (even if it's a missing pink marker from Ms. Kratzer's desk)

2. Behavior is a Science and Management is a Skill, So Don't Think it is Innate Instinct

- study the best

- get a role model in your head

- pretend you are them until you get it down pat (I used to pretend to be a mix of Black Mamba from the Kill Bill movies and an old, wise, unbreakable grandmother)

How to Do It :

1. Pavlov's Dog: Treat them the way they have been treated all their lives, otherwise they just won't respond to anything you say or do, after you have established a relationship then you can start to help them.

- ❖ In my first year, I made the mistake of wanting to adopt all of my students and they took advantage. Now, I wait for the right time to start the caring that comes along with spending hours upon hours with these little munchkins.

2. The first day of school is crucial

❖ I have my students act out the procedures of the classroom and make notes of the ones who follow directions and those that do not. This is only the beginning so you need to be CONSISTENT. Work on the ones who don't even follow directions on the first day. There's your project for the year.

3. Know your audience before you walk in (English proficiency, nationality, and reputation)

❖ The day I was hired, the principal asked me if I was comfortable teaching children of different nationalities. Sure I said, thinking "I'm not a racist, are we so rare?" Then, when I walk into my first day of school, none of the kids could speak English in my program.

4. learn Spanish and one or two words in the other languages, know the top three popular songs of the moment, and learn any slang used on an unanimous basis

❖ Then you start to realize the poetry of it all… "I'm a snuff you!" They are going to kill me, like a candle light being snuffed out. Brilliant!

* I earn their respect by trying to learn how they talk, in turn; they earn my respect by trying to learn. They want to be heard just like any other person and it's nice when they can express themselves in their everyday dialect and you "get" what they're saying.

5. In the first two months, take no prisoners. Be a complete and unfaltering Terminator machine to each and every one of them (you don't want to look soft).

When you earn each other's respect then you can begin to nurture them.

❖　　The best two days of my teaching career concerning behavior management were in October and May of my second year of teaching.

L.J. was part of the tougher yet manageable group in my hardest class. All 33 of them were testing me though. I never gave them an inch and provided great evidence of them not trying. A slip of paper that is filled out by the student stating their name, class, the assignment given, and their reason for not handing it in on time. They bake in a small blue binder until its time for parent teacher conferences. *DING! GET IT WHILE ITS HOT. I GOT EXCUSES COMING OUT OF THE WAZOO, ANY TAKERS?* Also, I used my support on the floor I was teaching on that day... the dean, the AP, their other teachers, and their mommas. Two months of this and then the day came when I knew I had them by "the balls" so to speak.

> **Ms.? Yo Ms.!**
> *Ms. What?*
> **Ms. Green**
> *What is your question?*
> **Well, we was wonderin if you were married?**
> *Nope, why?*
> **Because you're too tight, you needs to get laaaiiidddd.**

The month of May is glorious. The student's hearts and yours melt with the snow. The students have

13

finally stopped testing your limits and make astonishing strides in class work and group work. Then, without even realizing it, the eyes in the back of your head are peaking out from your shell of hair. You can spot an incident 5 seconds before it happens. With my back to all 33 of them I am writing on the chart paper. I hear the unmistakable sound of crinkling paper then giggles. *Don't even think about throwing paper balls, boys.* Without pausing I stopped a ruckus and earned respect in one swoop of a marker. At the end of the period Rosa stayed after to talk to me, like she has been for months now. Offering to carry binders for me, with much gratitude, I lead the way up the stairs. **Ms. Green thanks fo the grade third semesta, do you need help wid anythin else?** *Well, I do have my AK in my trunk maybe you can help with that after you eat lunch. Are you still coming up to the library after you eat?* **Damn Ms. Green! Stop playin round. Yeah, course I'll be dere, yous my nigga. Peace!**

What a compliment! Only her closest associates are referred to in this manner. I was now one of the few she trusted and has a deep connection with. Although she knows my feelings on the N- word she was trying to express herself. I tell them knowing the history of the African- Americans it offends ME even if it doesn't offend them.

6. They respect people who respect themselves (keep your posture straight, keep your chin up, hands folded in front of you, and dress in a style that makes you feel comfortable)

❖ There is the teacher who looks like he stepped out of Cape Cod...with his salmon colored slacks, cobalt blue button down, and color coordinated bow tie. However, the kids (and adults) respect him because he matches((very important) and he holds his own. BTW on that note, hooking up at work is like being a single parent because the stakes are that you will feel emotions that might interrupt the professional environment and the students might get caught up in the Game of Like. *I like you but let's be hush, hush about it...* formula for drama(I would know).

7. You are technically the legal guardian when in the classroom (do what you think is necessary to get the job done)

❖ When my students walk in the room they go to their assigned desk, stand behind it until they have taken out their notebook and pen to write down the essential question of the day, and then they can sit down

8. Find out who the ring leader is and make him/her your subordinate

* Apply peer pressure when the ringleader is M.I.A.

9. If there is situation, use physical presence to stop it

❖ Practice by walking across a Manhattan street when the walking sign gives you the cue. When the taxi makes a right hand turn across your path stare at the driver and keep walking the same pace. You are not running to get out of the way and you are not cursing and yelling at the taxi. You are calm and in control. You have the confidence to express the authority over the cabbie that **you** have the right of way and the taxi **will** abide by your decision.

* Never break up a fight! Just call the deans safety guards.

- Don't dial security unless there is blood or a student runs out of the room without permission (they're hardworking people, don't bother them with paper balls)

3. The Teaching Part of the Job Separates You from a Correctional Officer

- C.Y.A. (cover your ass)

- Don't fool yourself into thinking its going to be like how the media presents it. Little angels, sitting in rows, participating in class, and striving to succeed...because that's sure as hell not how it goes down **until** you master behavior management

- When you sign that contract, you are now a staff member of a city institution and your bosses, the union, the Board of Ed., the Mayor, the Governor, the three branches of government, and the citizens of this country all expect you to Leave No Child Behind!

How to Do it :

1. You can't do everything at once so get a feel for what you should prioritize on your To Do List (always keep a memo pad with you). Your social network can help you with this step.

2. If you are a Math or ELA teacher, your classroom should be your most important front (in the beginning people will judge you on how you adapt, its only natural, so prove yourself through your classroom…they even have a rubric for it)

3. Collect all copies of how your job performance will be assessed and in turn, you will be prepared (and at ease) when these assessments are made

i.e. Formal Observations by your supervisor, Lesson Plan Format, Classroom Environment, Bulletin Boards, Snapshots SEE GLOSSARY

4. It is <u>mandated</u> by the New York City Public School teachers to have <u>a lesson plan written out for every single lesson with you in the room</u>. I know, I know, this sounds weird. Why wouldn't you have a lesson? Well, imagine being so fucking tired you decide to just wing it a couple of times. The bright side is you can use the same lesson for different classes, just change the date and/or the content. Try to type your lessons. (Even if they are poor quality, due to lack of experience, it will look like you are a professional).

5. Use Technology.

❖ Use the internet for lessons, ideas, and examples. Throw in the webpage as a resource in your lesson plan if you up stand the laws of copyrighting. Technology- related projects for the students are huge these days.

6. Find out all the different resources for photocopying

❖ The copy machine reserved for teachers is 25 years old and then the photocopying service done by the photocopy woman, Christina, needs two days to get it done. Try to get on the good side of the supply manager at school. Staples and Kinko's will probably start to know you by name.

> *Keep track of who will help you so you don't abuse the privilege. This is also where Mr. Gomez's benevolence comes in; if you know the name of their husband, wife, kids, dog, something personable then they will do you that favor 99% of the time. Don't be douche about it though.

7. Use Edu-babble as much as possible. Talk the talk.

❖ You think data differentiation and the workshop model are useless. However, when discussing them, sigh and use an adage along the lines of "It is what it is"

8. Don't chalk n' talk. Use colorful charts, worksheets, and supplementary materials. SEE GLOSARRY

9. Go into other teacher's rooms during your off hours to watch them teach.

❖ Make sure to ask first, don't take any notes, and don't make it seem as though you are a spy for the higher- ups

10. When creating units, work backwards. Have a goal in mind and create the steps to get your students "there." The result should be one skill and one main idea that your students have learned. Seriously, just

one main idea from the unit they will remember at the end of the year is the minimum they should get out of it so be focused.

11. K.I.S.S. (Keep it simple, stupid)

❖ The perfect 42 minute lesson→ 1. Gain their interest by relating the topic to their lives. 2. Start out extra slow and then gain momentum with more information 3. Show a model of what the product should look like 4. Let them get to it, preferably in groups of four 5. Have two groups share with the whole class 6. Assign the HW, which should reinforce what they just learned or will lead them into tomorrow's lesson.

12. Use as many visuals as you can

❖ Don't be afraid to be a regular for borrowing the TV, computer lab, or Smart Board SEE GLOSSARY

> *If the movie is rated R, create a
> permission slip to show it in class

13. Create your own events to publicize your student's achievements

❖ The auditorium is under-used and other teachers are usually more than happy to take the period off from teaching

14. Find your own nook where no one can find you. Sometimes you need time to relax, reflect, grade, and plan at school. I suggest getting to school early and

leaving at dismissal. Some teachers like to get there at the last moment and stay after.

> * Do this only once a day because you should
>   still be maintaining your social network

15. Always have your schedule, the bell times, and a watch on your person. Also label everything that is yours...especially your stapler! Things have a habit of going missing.

Epilogue

The only thought to get me through that first year was, "I can't wait to tell these stories when I get over the hump of horror and can laugh about it." It only took me 8 months. In a place where up is down and left is right, you either spit or swallow. I decided to swallow and see where it took me. I am now an author at the same age as Winston Churchill when he published his first book… 25. Why am I often confused for being older than I am? I have gained the subdued now-it-all aura of a 55 year old. The hard work, sweat, tears, blood, shame, and fear all creep away when your character is being built day after day. You become a cool, calm, collected, inspirational, and many times cuddly human being. And my friend Chris? My buddy found love and has been traveling the dusty roads of America since he left bureaucracy behind two and half years ago.

Edu- babble

These phrases may seem obvious to some but as a teacher of the system, we are used to spelling everything out exactly so as not to cause misinterpretation.

Admin : the group of administrators that oversee a body of workers. They act as leaders, suck- ups, and critics

Aim : purpose of the lesson in a question

Assessment : term used for grading something or someone, various types

AP: assistant principal

Balanced Literacy: Balanced Literacy incorporates all reading approaches realizing students need to use multiple strategies to become proficient readers. It provides and cultivates the skills of reading, writing, thinking, speaking and listening for all students.

Board of Regents: Established by the New York State Legislature on May 1, 1784, the Regents of The University of the State of New York form the oldest, continuous state education entity in America. The Regents are responsible for the general supervision of all educational activities within the State, presiding over The University and the New York State Education Department. The Regents are organized into standing committees and subcommittees whose members and chairs are appointed by the Chancellor.

Chart : a 3 x 4 ft. piece of blank paper

Coverage : we get substitutes if the principal feels like shelling out the dough. Most of the time teachers get paid to cover absent teachers during their prep periods.

Data : information from tests to help you teach students to get better test scores

Dean : disciplinarian. May be more than one according to school size

Dept. of Ed. (formerly Board of Ed.): If this were 1971, it would be referred to as "The Man." the state education department in New York State. It is responsible for the supervision for all public schools in New York State and all standardized testing, as well as the production and administration of state tests and Regents Examinations. The main offices of the department are located in Albany, the state capital.

Differentiation : term used for teachers to cater to all the different levels of student's abilities in one lesson, usually solved by teaming up low level and high level students

DOE account : Microsoft Outlook e-mail account for all employees of the New York City school system

Fellow : The NYC Teaching Fellows are non- Education Bachelors college graduates who have decided to change their lives and teach in the classrooms that need teachers most. The majority of Fellows enter the program with little or no teaching experience.

File number : tattoo this on your body somewhere, this is similar to your social security # in this world

Formal observation : one of your supervisors will watch one of your lessons at a predetermined date, it will be graded on a rubric, and go in your file

Graphic Organizer : format for students to put ideas into an easy- to- categorize diagram. It often depicts the relationships between facts, terms, and or ideas within a learning task. It is often referred to as a "map" because it can help teachers and students "map out" their ideas in a visual manner. There are many similar names for graphic organizers including: knowledge maps, concept maps, story maps, cognitive organizers, advance organizers, or concept diagrams.

High level : smart kid

Independent study : may be initiated by student or teacher, the focus here will be on planned independent study by students under the guidance or supervision of a classroom teacher. In addition, independent study can include learning in partnership with another individual or as part of a small group.

Journal Writing: a learning tool based on the ideas that students write to learn. Students use the journals to write about topics of personal interest, to note their observations, to imagine, to wonder and to connect new information with things they already know.

Low level : not so smart kid

Model : show the students how you would like their project to turn out by showing them examples

Mutiple Intelligence Theory: There are at least 6 categories people can be intelligent in besides Math and English. The theory of multiple intelligences was developed in 1983 by Dr. Howard Gardner, professor of education at Harvard University. It suggests that the traditional notion of intelligence, based on I.Q. testing, is far too limited. Instead, Dr. Gardner proposes eight different intelligences to account for a broader range of human potential in children and adults.

NCLB : No Child Left Behind Act, Public Law 107–110. Educational rhetoric created by the Bush administration in 2001 to turn schools into factories through "teaching to the test." Benefits= every state will be teaching the same curriculum so there will be no deprived groups.

ODD: Oppositional Defiance Disorder. It is a psychiatric disorder that is characterized by two different sets of problems. These are aggressiveness and a tendency to purposefully bother and irritate others. Don't write off kids who are bothersome as having ODD, however, encourage ways of curbing it. Suggest that they eat healthy and exercise, limit TV and Video games, and then spend time getting to know them.

Objective : an outcome that the student <u>will</u> be able to do by the end of the lesson

Post- observation : about 3 days after your formal observation, you will receive feedback

Pre- observation : about 3 days before your formal observation, bring the lesson and materials you plan to use that day and receive feedback from your supervisor

Prep : Time planned in your program to prepare for elements of the teaching process or behavior management. You are guaranteed at least one prep period a day on top of your lunch period.

Program : Your classes, the periods you teach, and the classroom you teach in. You must teach in your certification

Project Based Learning Method: a comprehensive approach to instruction. Your students participate in projects and practice an interdisciplinary array of skills from math, language arts, fine arts, geography, science, and technology.

Read Aloud: A read aloud is a planned oral reading of a book or print excerpt, usually related to a theme or topic of study. The read aloud can be used to engage the student listener while developing background knowledge, increasing comprehension skills, and fostering critical thinking.

Rubric : In general a rubric is a scoring guide used in subjective assessments. A rubric implies that a rule defining the criteria of an assessment system is followed in evaluation. A rubric can be an explicit description of performance characteristics corresponding to a point on a rating scale. A scoring rubric makes explicit expected qualities of performance on a rating scale or the definition of a single scoring point on a scale.

*Formal observation rubric N= needs improvement, M= meets criteria, and E= exceeds criteria

Security: the 2 police officers stationed at the front entrance for emergency situations

Snapshot: a legal observation, one of your supervisors will watch one of your lessons at an unprecedented date, it will be graded on a rubric, and go in your file

Standards: State curriculum outcomes created by the Board of Regents. They represent the core of what all people should know, understand and be able to do as a result of their schooling.

Standardized Testing: The tests are designed in such a way that the "questions, conditions for administering, scoring procedures, and interpretations are consistent" and are "administered and scored in a predetermined, standard manner.

Supplementary materials: everything but a textbook * this includes worksheets, projects supplies, and charts

Teacher- student conferences: sit down with students individually, dish about what they're learning, record it in the appropriate teacher conference format

Teacher's Choice: $140 dollars worth of receipts to be spent on teaching materials. Which might be a fourth of what you do end up shelling out.

TFA: (Teach for America) white bread chicks and dudes trying to save the world. They come from the Midwest and are stationed in the poorest sections of major cities the two years they have to get their free Masters degree.

Tweed : building used as the NYC Board of Ed. central location

*The building was named for William M. "Boss" Tweed, who ran a notoriously tyrannical governorship in the 1850's

UFT: United Federal of Teachers. The sole bargaining agent for most of the non-supervisory educators who work in the New York City public schools. Your chapter leader can advise you on the laws and contract rules when in time of need.

"Your file": a threatening item used by your supervisors to keep a log of your teaching practices

Phone Numbers

Let's just say you should write the first name of the student and then list his/her last name. Then, first and last name of the *father, mother, grandmother, grandfather, parole officer, aunt, uncle, and/or siblings.*

A

B

C

D

E

F

G

H

I

J

K

L

M

N

○

P

Q

R

S

T

U

V

Y

z

Gwendolyn Green is the pseudonym used by a teacher of 4 years in the New York Public School System in a low income and highly diverse section of the Bronx. She has been a resident of the state of New York for 23 years and thought it would be a great idea when in high school, out in the suburbs, that she would like to be teacher. She received her B.A. in education from Manhattan College in Riverdale, NY. Although an outstanding and wealthy section, it is still technically part of the Boogie Down Bronx. Most of the college's connections (its all who you know -FYI) are in that borough. In conclusion, the author was offered a position to teach at a tidy and heavily beaurocratic school and has since gone gray both from genetics and stress.